Whispers of The Soul

Whispers of The Soul

By: Sheila M. Burke

Om Sweet Om Publishing
Seven Hills, Ohio

Om Sweet Om Publishing

Printed and bound in the United States

Cover design by Sheila M. Burke © 2013
All photographs and quotes © Sheila M. Burke

ISBN-13: 978-0615769516 (Om Sweet Om)

ISBN-10: 0615769519

Library of Congress Card Number – Pending
Whispers of The Soul / Sheila M. Burke
ISBN 0615769519
1st Edition

www.ZenSationalLiving.com

Dedicated to my Muse
and to all the soul connections
I have found in this lifetime.

Did you ever meet someone and become fast friends, where you feel as if you have known them your entire life, although you've only just met recently? I know those feelings well; I have them on occasion. I think they are leftover energies, imprints if you will, left upon the universe from times past. A wink and smile and perhaps a bond from another time that went deep. Coming full circle and finding you again in this lifetime.

The energy of spirit and soul is not breakable – you will find people over and over again in your journey, in one form or another whether they are lovers, friends, or family.
The label you put on those relationships does not matter in the least – it's the bond of love, of spirit – that finds its way back together through universal connections in lifetimes. These are our soul connections.

When we experience these uncanny feelings of having known someone before, when relationships are experienced as heightened through each of our senses, when you feel as if you are being pulled or guided ~ these are the **Whispers of The Soul.**

EVERYTHING WE DO IN OUR TIME HERE LEAVES AN IMPRINT.

AN IMPRINT UPON THE UNIVERSE FOR ALL ETERNITY.

THIS IS WHY A COMPLETE STRANGER MIGHT FEEL UNCANNILY FAMILIAR.

IT'S THE REASON WHY WE OCCASIONALLY FEEL STRONG CONNECTIONS TO

PEOPLE WE'VE NEVER MET BEFORE;

RESIDUAL ENERGY FROM LONG AGO DAYS;

RELATIONSHIPS LONG FORGOTTEN ~

finding their way back together ~ to warm your soul.

Sheila M. Burke, Zen-Sational Living

Your Spirit, Your Soul,
SPEAKS AS YOU SHIFT FROM CONSCIOUS
SELF TO SUBCONSCIOUS SELF.
A VOICE EXPRESSED THROUGH DREAMS;
A GIFT OF INSIGHT PRESENTED
THROUGH COINCIDENCE;
A FLIGHT TAKEN OFF
THROUGH YOUR HEART.

Sheila M. Burke

Even the old souls may take the longer, more difficult road to where they belong, but deep down they have faith in knowing they'll end up where they are meant to be.

Eventually.

SOMETIMES YOU JUST HAVE TO TAKE
A LEAP OF FAITH AND ALLOW
YOURSELF TO BE GUIDED BY
SOMETHING BIGGER THAN YOU.
Listen to your Soul

THERE IS NO WISER THING FOR
YOU TO DO IN THIS LIFETIME
THEN TO LET YOUR SOUL GUIDE
YOU, AS THE SOUL IS THE ONLY
REASON YOU ARE HERE.

When you find something genuine...

an uncanny feeling that pulses through your veins propelled by the very force of the universe... when each and every sense is awakened purely by thought... When every capillary, every cell, every fiber is touched within you ... when you have an ache deep down into your bones, wrapping itself around your breath, and dancing through each and every heartbeat... close your eyes and let it envelop your entire Being. This is your Soul speaking to you, be still. Listen.

SHEILA BURKE ZEN-SATIONAL LIVING

I feel you in every breath;
as the cool wind dances upon my cheek;
in the sound of the waves rushing over the sand.
Each soft ray of sunshine allows me to close
my eyes and imagine you here with me.

You nourish my Soul.

There are no accidental meetings between souls.

Well, I don't know about you but...

I AM NOT GOING TO FIND MYSELF IN THE SUNSET OF MY LIFE WONDERING ABOUT A CHANCE NOT TAKEN, AN OPPORTUNITY MISSED, OR A FEELING NOT FOLLOWED. MY HEART SHALL GO THE WAY OF MY SOUL, *for my Soul* IS THE REASON I AM HERE.

SHEILA M. BURKE

You'll never know what life holds
if you don't give in and have a taste.

There are no coincidences.
It is your soul...
whispering to you in dreams,
during waking hours,
and in quiet moments.
Leading you; shining for you;
a beacon home.

Finding the missing piece doesn't change the mosaic. It completes it, makes it whole.

If it doesn't nourish
your soul, get rid of it.

When beautiful possibilities
fall upon your path
don't step over them.
Appreciate the odds involved with the
Universe placing these two things
together at that very moment.

I believe in song. I believe a song in your ear can take you to a far away place. I believe a song in your heart can lead you to somewhere you would never intended on going ~ yet understand that it is your destination. I BELIEVE IN EITHER CASE YOU CAN LISTEN OR TUNE THEM OUT. I ALSO BELIEVE YOU WILL KEEP HEARING YOUR SONG UNTIL YOU *close your eyes* AND *open your heart* TO THE MELODY OF YOUR SOUL.

SHEILA BURKE ZEN-SATIONAL LIVING

Sometimes you fall down, because there is something down there that you are supposed to find.

The Spirit and Soul
are a dynamic duo.
Step out from your mind ~
let them lead the way.

Every choice you make plays a different
song in your heart, but when you fail
to pick up the instrument,
you will not hear the tune.

Sheila M. Burke

The
journey is
much easier
when you are

not carrying

your past.

Will you
listen to the
chaos in your mind

or the whisper
of your
heart?

HOW IN THE WORLD
WILL YOU EVER GET TO WHERE
YOU ARE GOING... IF YOU FAIL TO TAKE
CHANCES AND FOLLOW YOUR HEART?
THAT EXCITEMENT THAT FLOWS
THROUGH YOUR VEINS IS SPIRITUAL
ENERGY - PULLING YOU, GUIDING YOU.

IT WHISPERS *follow me.*

Sheila M. Burke

I believe in truth.

I BELIEVE FEELINGS CAN CHANGE.

I BELIEVE YOU CAN BE MOVING HAPPILY ALONG

IN LIFE WHEN SUDDENLY YOU FIND YOURSELF

SOMEWHERE ELSE ~ SOMEWHERE YOU WOULD

RATHER BE. SOMEWHERE YOU WERE MEANT TO BE.

SOMEWHERE YOU WERE GUIDED TO BE.

I BELIEVE IN MAKING THE MOST *of what*
the Universe presents to us.

SHEILA M. BURKE ZEN-SATIONAL LIVING

All energy is intertwined.
Life carried on within,
yet affecting all that is touched by it.

I believe in true love.

The kind of love that wraps
it's cosmic fingers around your
very soul. Deeply engaging
each of your senses. I believe this
is a once in a lifetime connection
sent from another time and space.
Seeking you out,
pulling you in, whispering

"Oh, I've missed you so".

Sheila M. Burke Zen-Sational Living

www.ingramcontent.com/pod-product-compliance
Lightning Source LLC
Chambersburg PA
CBHW040232070426
42447CB00030B/160